GREAT AMERICAN
MUSCLE CARS
AN IMAGINATION LIBRARY SERIES

Cobras

ERIC ETHAN

Gareth Stevens Publishing
MILWAUKEE

For a free color catalog describing Gareth Stevens Publishing's list of high-quality books and multimedia programs, call 1-800-542-2595 (USA) or 1-800-461-9120 (Canada). Gareth Stevens Publishing's Fax: (414) 225-0377. See our catalog, too, on the World Wide Web: http://gsinc.com

Library of Congress Cataloging-in-Publication Data

Ethan, Eric.
    Cobras / by Eric Ethan.
      p. cm. — (Great American muscle cars—an imagination library series.
    Includes index.
    Summary: Surveys the history of the Shelby Cobra and its designs, engines, performance, and costs.
    ISBN 0-8368-1743-5 (lib. bdg.)
    1. Cobra automobile—Juvenile literature. [1. Cobra automobile.]
I. Title. II. Series: Ethan, Eric. Great American muscle cars—an imagination library series.
TL215.C566E84   1998
629.222'2—dc21   97-31770

First published in North America in 1998 by
Gareth Stevens Publishing
1555 North RiverCenter Drive, Suite 201
Milwaukee, WI 53212 USA

This edition © 1998 by Gareth Stevens, Inc. Text by Eric Ethan. Photographs by Ron Kimball (cover, pages 5, 11, 15, 17, 19, and 21) and Nicky Wright (pages 7, 9, and 13). Additional end matter © 1998 by Gareth Stevens, Inc.

Text: Eric Ethan
Page layout: Eric Ethan, Helene Feider
Cover design: Helene Feider
Series design: Shari Tikus

Printed in the United States of America

1 2 3 4 5 6 7 8 9 02 01 00 99 98

TABLE OF CONTENTS

Words that appear in the glossary are printed in **boldface** type the first time they occur in the text.

THE FIRST COBRAS

Most people think the Cobra sports car was an American design. The first Cobras, however, were built in England by a company called AC Cars.

Carroll Shelby, an American race car driver, believed the English Cobra could be improved. Shelby began bringing AC cars to America.

He replaced the original Cobra engine with a much larger one made by Ford. The first Ford-powered Cobras rolled out of Shelby's Los Angeles (California) factory in 1962. The Shelby Cobra is America's rarest factory-made muscle car.

Muscle cars are American-made, two-door sports **coupes** *with powerful engines made for high-performance driving. This 1965 AC Cobra shows the clean design of the original British car that was later modified by Carroll Shelby.*

WHAT DO COBRAS LOOK LIKE?

Cobras are low-riding, two-seat sports cars. Most of the space is taken up by the engine. Passengers sit far to the rear, overlooking a long hood. The original English sports car design is easy to see — round fenders and a smooth **airflow** were common on English sports cars of the time.

When Shelby Cobras were first sold, they reminded people of Corvettes. Until 1962, the Corvette, an all-American design, had a similar look. But after 1962, the Corvette was redesigned and became much more **angular**. The Cobra body style changed very little during the entire time it was manufactured.

The 1966 Cobra was a powerful-looking car.

WHAT WAS THE FASTEST COBRA?

The first Shelby Cobras built in 1962 were very fast. They featured a 289-cubic-inch (4.7-liter) Ford engine. The greater the cubic inches, the faster the car. Cobras with this engine did very well on the racetrack.

In 1964, Shelby took the Cobra a step further. A huge 427-cubic-inch (7-liter) Ford racing motor was put in place. Such a powerful engine in a small body produced an amazingly fast race car. Anyone who wanted to could buy a 427-cubic-inch (7-liter) Cobra from Shelby. But it was more car than anyone except a **professional** race car driver could handle. Many of the people who bought Cobras went to Carroll Shelby's driving school in Riverside, California. There they learned to drive these powerful cars safely.

*Shelby put a 427-cubic-inch (7-liter) Ford **stock car** racing motor into this small, two-seat Cobra.*

COBRA ENGINES

The 427-cubic-inch (7-liter) Ford engine barely fit under the Cobra hood. There was no room to spare in the Cobra engine **compartment**. Ford had planned to put the 427-cubic-inch (7-liter) engine into large stock cars.

On top of the engine is a large **carburetor**. Carburetors take air into the engine. Racing engines need a lot of air to run at high speed. An **air scoop** on the car's hood forces air into the carburetor. The air is mixed with gasoline in the car's engine. The mixture is burned to power the car.

Once the 427-cubic-inch (7-liter) Ford racing motor was squeezed into the Cobra's engine compartment, there was not much room left.

COBRA INTERIORS

The Cobra is a small car. Its passenger compartment is a tight fit for most people. Cobras are so short that drivers sit ahead of the gear box. This means the gear shift lever has to be bent forward.

Both the steering wheel and instruments are on the right side of the car. That is the way cars like the AC were made in England. Sometimes Shelby would move the steering wheel and instruments to the left side to match American cars. But some customers wanted it left the way it was originally made.

Can you see the Cobra logo in the center of the steering wheel and on the trunk that Shelby added to his cars?

COBRAS RACING

Most American car companies build race cars to help sell their regular models, but all Cobras were fast cars. To make them winning racers, very little needed to be added.

The Cobra pictured has special equipment to make it safer and faster to race. Wider tires were added in the rear so that all the power reached the road. Large **exhaust** pipes that help the engine breathe better and run faster were also added.

The numbers on the door do not make the car go any faster. But they help identify this car as a very special Cobra.

Most Cobra owners need only add special tires and exhaust pipes to convert a factory standard car into a winning racer.

BEAUTIFUL COBRAS

Great care was taken with the Cobra to make a beautiful, hand-finished car. Very few Cobras were made, and they were expensive cars.

People who bought the Cobra wanted a car that looked good. Shelby never disappointed them. The original AC design with **accessories** added by Shelby pleased the customers. Cobras always made an impression. Movie stars bought them, and songs were written about them.

Even though the Shelby Cobra was a beautiful race car, it was also a very good street car.

In 1966, the Ford Cobra reached its peak of power and functional design.

THE LAST COBRAS

The last Shelby Cobras rolled out of the Los Angeles plant in March of 1967. During the five years of production, just over a thousand Cobras were made. Fans of the Cobra like to point out that the last ones built were even faster and handled better than the first ones. The Cobra got better and better until the end.

It is difficult to be a successful **custom** sports car manufacturer. The Cobra made a big impact on the racetrack and the public, but there were few paying customers for such a fast car. By 1967, Shelby had begun another program with Ford. Together, they made special Shelby versions of the Mustang that were also very fast.

Pictured is one of the last Cobras (a 427) made in 1967 at the Carroll Shelby plant in Los Angeles.

WHAT DID COBRAS COST?

Cobras were expensive cars for their time. A Cobra with a 427-cubic-inch (7-liter) engine intended for use on the street could cost over $6,000. Only Corvettes, America's other two-seat sports car, cost as much.

Very few **options** were available on Cobras. The basic car that AC originally delivered to Shelby did not change very much from 1962 to 1967. Shelby added the engine, **transmission**, paint, and a few accessories. What the customer received for the money was a **legendary** automobile.

*Out of production since 1967, the Cobra lives on in **repli-cars**, like the one pictured. Repli-cars reproduce the classic lines of the original Shelby automobiles.*

WHAT DO COBRAS COST TODAY?

Anyone who bought an original Cobra and kept it is very fortunate. The value of Cobras has gone up more than any other recently made American car. Part of the reason is that very few were manufactured.

Some of the originals, of course, no longer exist. The ones that remain can sell for up to forty times the original price. People who want to buy a Cobra today have difficulty finding one for sale.

Many people purchase a copy of the Cobra in a **kit car**. The kit car has a body that looks like a Cobra, but it goes on the **chassis** of another car of similar size. Nearly as many kit-car Cobras have been sold as the original Shelby Cobras.

GLOSSARY

accessories (ak-SESS-or-eze) — Objects that provide comfort or decoration.

air scoop — The part of a car that forces air into the carburetor.

airflow (EHR-flow) — The motion of air around an object that is immersed in air.

angular (ANG-u-ler) — Having one or more sharp corners.

carburetor (CAR-burr-ay-ter) — The part of a car that supplies the engine with an explosive, vaporized fuel-air mixture.

chassis (CHA-see) — The frame that the rest of a car is built on.

compartment (kom-PART-ment) — A separate area surrounded by four walls or sides.

coupe (koop) — An enclosed, two-door automobile that is smaller than a sedan.

custom (KUS-tum) — Manufactured according to a customer's personal and special order.

exhaust (ig-ZOST) — The escape of used gas or vapor from an engine.

kit car — A car that is a copy of an original design. The body looks like the original, but it is placed on the chassis of another car.

legendary (LEG-en-dare-ee) — Well known or famous.

option (OP-shun) — A feature that can be added over and above the other features.

professional (pro-FESH-eh-nul) — A person who earns money for participating in a certain activity.

repli-car (REP-lih car) — A close and similar reproduction of a car.

stock car — A racing car with the basic chassis of an assembly-line model.

transmission (TRANS-mih-shun) — The part of a car that transfers the engine's power to the axle and wheels.

WEB SITES

www.xs4all.nl/~luukb/

www.carrollshelby.com

www.inlink.com/~jwinkler

www.cobracountry.com/

PLACES TO WRITE

Classic Motorbooks
729 Prospect Avenue, P.O. Box 1
Osceola, WI 54020 1-800-826-6600

Shelby American Automobile Club
P.O. Box 788
Sharon, CT 06069
e-mail: saac@ll.com

Carroll Shelby Enterprises
19021 South Figueroa Street
Gardena, CA 90248

Kit Car Illustrated
774 South Placentia
Placentia, CA 92870-6832

INDEX